I LOVE TO GO TO DAYCARE
ICH GEHE GERN IN DIE KITA

A bilingual book

Shelley Admont

Illustrated by Sonal Goyal, Sumit Sakhuja

www.kidkiddos.com

Copyright©2014 by S.A.Publishing ©2017 by KidKiddos Books Ltd.

support@kidkiddos.com

All rights reserved. No part of this book may be reproduced in any form or by any electronic or mechanical means, including information storage and retrieval systems, without written permission from the publisher or author, except in the case of a reviewer, who may quote brief passages embodied in critical articles or in a review.
Second edition, 2020

Translated from English by Tess Parthum
Aus dem Englischen übersetzt von Tess Parthum

Library and Archives Canada Cataloguing in Publication
I love to Go to Daycare (German Bilingual Edition)/ Shelley Admont
ISBN: 978-1-5259-2290-9 paperback
ISBN: 978-1-77268-505-3 hardcover
ISBN: 978-1-77268-110-9 ebook

Please note that the German and English versions of the story have been written to be as close as possible. However, in some cases they differ in order to accommodate nuances and fluidity of each language.

For those I love the most-S.A.
Für die, die ich am meisten liebe-S.A.

Jimmy was lying in his bed hugging his favorite teddy bear. He was really trying to sleep, but something bothered him and kept him wide awake.

Jimmy lag in seinem Bett und umarmte seinen Lieblings-Teddybären. Er versuchte zu schlafen, aber etwas quälte ihn und hielt ihn wach.

He rolled out of bed and went to look for his parents.

Er rollte aus dem Bett und ging auf die Suche nach seinen Eltern.

Down in the living room, his mom and dad were watching TV. Holding his teddy, Jimmy sat on Mom's lap. "Mommy, I can't sleep," he said.

Unten im Wohnzimmer sahen seine Mama und sein Papa gerade fern. Mit seinem Teddy im Arm setzte sich Jimmy auf Mamas Schoß. „Mami, ich kann nicht schlafen", sagte er.

Mom ruffled his hair and gave him a kiss. "What are you thinking about?"

Mama zerzauste sein Haar und gab ihm einen Kuss. „Woran denkst du?"

"I'm thinking about daycare," he whispered and hugged Mom tightly.

„Ich denke an die Kita", flüsterte er und drückte Mama fest.

"Oh, sweetie, daycare is so fun!" said Mom.

„Oh Schatz, die Kita macht so viel Spaß!", sagte Mama.

"You'll meet new friends there," added Dad. "In fact, it's so much fun that I wish I could go, too!"

„Du wirst dort neue Freunde kennenlernen", fügte Papa hinzu. „Es macht sogar so viel Spaß, dass ich mir wünsche, ich könnte auch mitgehen!"

"Can I stay at home with you?" asked Jimmy. His head fell on Mom's shoulder.

„Kann ich mit dir zuhause bleiben?", fragte Jimmy. Sein Kopf fiel auf Mamas Schulter.

Mom stroked his head, looking deeply into his eyes.

Mama streichelte seinen Kopf und schaute tief in seine Augen.

"How about this," she said. "Since it's your first day in daycare, you'll only stay there for two hours. After that, I'll come back to take you home. But I'm sure that you'll have so much fun that you won't even want to leave."

„Wie wäre es damit", sagte sie. „Weil es dein erster Tag in der Kita ist, wirst du nur für zwei Stunden dort bleiben. Danach komme ich wieder, um dich nach Hause zu bringen. Aber ich bin mir sicher, dass du so viel Spaß haben wirst, dass du gar nicht gehen wollen wirst."

"You know what?" said Dad. "You can even take your teddy bear with you. Does that sound good?" Jimmy nodded.

„Weißt du was?", sagte Papa. „Du kannst sogar deinen Teddybären mitnehmen. Hört sich das gut an?" Jimmy nickte.

"Oh, you're such a big and smart boy," said Mom, kissing his forehead. "I'm sure you're tired. Let's go to bed."

„Oh, du bist so ein großer und schlauer Junge", murmelte Mama und küsste seine Stirn. „Ich bin sicher, du bist müde. Lass uns ins Bett gehen."

She led Jimmy to his room and tucked him in. Then, she gave him a goodnight kiss and whispered in his ear, "I love you, sweetie."

Sie brachte Jimmy in sein Zimmer und deckte ihn zu. Dann gab sie ihm einen Gute-Nacht-Kuss und flüsterte in sein Ohr: „Ich habe dich lieb, Schatz."

"I love you too, Mom," said Jimmy. With a big yawn, he hugged his teddy bear and closed his eyes.

„Ich habe dich auch lieb, Mama", sagte Jimmy. Mit einem großen Gähnen umarmte er seinen Teddybären und schloss seine Augen.

Jimmy was almost asleep when he heard a strange voice. "Hey, Jimmy!"

Jimmy war schon fast eingeschlafen, als er eine fremde Stimme hörte. „Hey, Jimmy!"

He opened his eyes, looking around. "Who's talking?" murmured Jimmy.

Er öffnete seine Augen und schaute umher. „Wer spricht da?", murmelte Jimmy.

"It's me, your teddy bear!"

„Ich bin es, dein Teddybär!"

Astonished, Jimmy looked down. The teddy bear waved his hand and smiled. "I saw you were upset," said the teddy bear.

Erstaunt schaute Jimmy nach unten. Der Teddybär winkte und lächelte. „Ich habe gesehen, dass du aufgewacht warst", sagte der Teddybär.

Jimmy sighed deeply. "Yes, I'm going to daycare tomorrow," he mumbled.
Jimmy seufzte tief. „Ja, ich gehe morgen in die Kita", murmelte er.

"Jimmy, my friend, but I'm going with you!" The teddy bear winked at Jimmy and gave him his big teddy-bear smile.
„Jimmy, mein Freund, aber ich gehe doch mit dir!" Der Teddybär zwinkerte ihm zu und schenkte ihm sein großes Teddybären-Lächeln.

Jimmy looked at him jumping and clapping and burst out laughing.
Jimmy schaute ihm zu, springend und klatschend und brach in Gelächter aus.

"Shhhh," whispered the teddy bear. He pointed to Jimmy's two older brothers, who were sleeping in their beds.
„Pssst", flüsterte der Teddybär. Er zeigte auf Jimmys zwei ältere Brüder, die in ihren Betten schliefen.

The next morning his two older brothers jumped out of bed and walked over to Jimmy.

Am nächsten Morgen sprangen seine beiden älteren Brüder aus dem Bett und gingen zu Jimmy.

"Today is your first day in daycare. You are so lucky," said his oldest brother.

„Heute ist dein erster Tag in der Kita. Du hast so ein Glück", sagte sein ältester Bruder.

Jimmy was excited but a little bit worried. "I'm only going for two hours today," he murmured. "Is it a long time?"

Jimmy war aufgeregt, aber ein bisschen besorgt. „Ich gehe heute nur für zwei Stunden", murmelte er. „Ist das eine lange Zeit?"

"Not really," said the oldest brother.
"You won't even stay for a nap," added the middle brother.

„Nicht wirklich", sagte der älteste Bruder. „Du wirst nicht mal bis zum Mittagsschlaf bleiben", fügte der mittlere Bruder hinzu.

During breakfast Jimmy was very quiet. "Are you ready to go, Jimmy?" Mom asked, after he cleared his plate.

Während des Frühstücks war Jimmy sehr still. „Bist du bereit zu gehen, Jimmy?", fragte Mama, nachdem er seinen Teller geleert hatte.

"I guess," he answered looking down at his teddy bear.

„Ich denke schon", antwortete er und schaute hinunter auf seinen Teddybären.

The teddy bear gave him a big smile and Jimmy felt much better.

Der Teddybär lächelte ihn groß an und Jimmy fühlte sich viel besser.

He took his teddy bear in one hand and Mommy's hand in the other and they set out.

Er nahm seinen Teddybären in die eine Hand und Mamas Hand in die andere und sie machten sich auf den Weg.

"You'll like it, honey," said Mom while they were walking. "And I'll be back in two hours, right after snack time."

„Es wird dir gefallen, Liebling", sagte Mama, während sie liefen. „Und ich werde in zwei Stunden zurück sein, direkt nach dem Essen."

"I know, Mommy. I'm fine. I have my teddy bear with me." Jimmy winked at his bear.

„Ich weiß, Mami. Mir geht es gut. Ich habe meinen Teddybären bei mir." Jimmy zwinkerte seinem Bären zu.

"I'm so proud of you, my big boy," said Mom as the pair walked up to the daycare's door.

„Ich bin so stolz auf dich, mein großer Junge", sagte Mama, als die beiden zur Tür der Kita hinaufgingen.

Mom knocked twice, and a lady appeared at the door.
Mama klopfte zweimal an und eine Frau erschien an der Tür.

"Hello, Jimmy," the lady said. "Come on in!"
„Hallo, Jimmy", sagte die Frau. „Komm herein!"

"How does she know me?" Jimmy whispered to his mom.
„Woher kennt sie mich?", flüsterte Jimmy seiner Mama zu.

Mom smiled. "I called her before and told her we were coming."
Mama lächelte. „Ich habe sie vorher angerufen und ihr gesagt, dass wir kommen."

There were a lot of other kids there. Some of them were playing with cars, and others were playing with dolls.
Es waren viele andere Kinder dort. Einige von ihnen spielten mit Autos und andere spielten mit Puppen.

"Let's go have some fun. Come on, Jimmy!" the teddy bear said. Smiling, Jimmy turned to Mom.

„Lass uns gehen und Spaß haben. Komm schon, Jimmy!", sagte der Teddybär. Lächelnd drehte sich Jimmy zu Mama um.

"Go have fun, sweetie," she said. "I'll pick you up right after snack time."

„Geh und hab Spaß, Schatz", sagte sie. „Ich hole dich gleich nach dem Essen ab."

"I remember. Bye, Mom!" Jimmy yelled as he ran to play with a large truck.

„Ich weiß. Tschüss, Mama!", rief Jimmy, als er losrannte, um mit einem großen Truck zu spielen.

After two hours, Mom came back to the daycare to pick up Jimmy. He ran to meet her and gave her a huge hug.

Nach zwei Stunden kam Mama zurück, um Jimmy aus der Kita abzuholen. Er rannte los, um sie zu treffen und gab ihr eine große Umarmung.

"Mom, it was so much fun!" he shouted. "I played with a large truck, and then I painted a flower for you all by myself!"

„Mama, es hat so viel Spaß gemacht!", schrie er. „Ich habe mit einem großen Truck gespielt und dann habe ich ganz allein eine Blume für dich gemalt!"

Mom smiled happily. "It's so beautiful. What else did you do today?"

Mama lächelte glücklich. „Sie ist so schön. Was hast du heute noch gemacht?"

"The teacher read us a book, and after that we ate a snack," Jimmy said in one breath, bouncing near Mom.

„Die Lehrerin hat uns ein Buch vorgelesen und danach haben wir eine Kleinigkeit gegessen", sagte Jimmy in einem Atemzug und hüpfte neben Mama.

"Can I stay for longer tomorrow? Please, Mom!"

„Kann ich morgen länger bleiben? Bitte, Mama!"

The next day, he stayed longer. The day after that he stayed even longer.
Am nächsten Tag blieb er länger. Am Tag danach blieb er sogar noch länger.

Now, Jimmy spends the whole day in daycare having lots of fun! He loves to play games and paint, to hear stories and eat.
Jetzt verbringt Jimmy den ganzen Tag in der Kita und hat viel Spaß! Er spielt gern Spiele und malt gern, er hört gern Geschichten und isst gern.

He is also happy when naptime comes, so he can rest a little bit.
Er freut sich auch, wenn es Zeit ist für den Mittagsschlaf, damit er sich ein wenig ausruhen kann.

Sometimes Jimmy doesn't bring teddy bear with him.
Manchmal nimmt Jimmy den Teddybären nicht mit.

But when he comes back home from daycare, Jimmy tells him all about his day.
Aber wenn Jimmy aus der Kita nach Hause kommt, erzählt er ihm alles von seinem Tag.

www.ingramcontent.com/pod-product-compliance
Lightning Source LLC
LaVergne TN
LVHW072113060526
838200LV00061B/4880